Poetry from Algernon

Algernon Trousdale

ACKNOWLEDGEMENT

Algernon would like to thank their life partner, family, and friends for the space to create and be challenged to write in this way.

PREFACE

21 days
  To find the ways
To write about anything poetic
A challenge to put words and letters
  To g e t h e r
Mean i n g f u l l y
  To evoke

Let the challenge begin…

silence screams

silence screams
if you pay attention
it screams the words
that fear won't mention

words both silent and loud
collectively make a sound
so much like
apprehension

when a hesitant tone
belies what is known
it can be a sore
source of contention

much can be told
by the eyes
can be caught by the look
of surprise

for silence to end
all actions must tend
away from all kinds
of pretension

compassion speaks out
without trying to shout
with an end to the
silent dimension

Ode to Haiku

I challenged myself
To write for 21 days
Poetry. Here. Now.

Will I find me here?
As I write my thoughts out loud?
Multitasking, too?

Half-thoughts in my head
While thinking of what to say
Haiku ideas

Why am I here, now?
Why am I writing haiku?
M e t a analyze

Philosophize life
Ask all important questions
Poetically

21 Haiku
Determined to write it out
And see where this goes

Sleep, rest and recharge.

Then explore what lies within.
Amidst other things.

What is poetry?
What rules are there to follow?
Writing Haiku time

S-O-C-K-S
Is something to learn to say
Spanish acceptance

It is what it is
When your life gives you lemons
You learn to squeeze them

All paradoxes
Are rooted in only one
Sword with two edges

Can you hold one thought
While imagining nothing?
Mindfulness practice

Forgetting one's self
Is a courageous venture
A new one comes out

Lots of things to do
Too much; no time for haiku

Stopped to write this down

Promises I made
Promises I want to keep
Nothing gets broken

Productive day, yay!
These need to happen often
Mindfulness abounds

There are 5 more left
And after this will be 4
Ode to haiku poems

My favorite ones
Because the poems are odd
Three, five, and seven

Opportunity
What gets left behind for it?
Sacrifice yourself

Almost to the end
Of this written haiku ode
What did it reveal

Creativity
21 Haiku are done
Time moves forward still

Untitled

Having too much to think about
Sometimes feels like a chain
Around my neck
Dragging me down
By
   m
     y

       t
        h
         o
         u
         g
        h
        t
         s

Three Sides

I have seen
All three sides
Of circumstance

I have been
All three sides
Of perspective

I once spoke ill of another
And heard ill spoken of another
Then saw how another responded
When ill was spoken of me

I have felt betrayal by another
And have betrayed another
Then witnessed another betrayed
But did nothing

Why do we hurt?
Why do we hurt each other?
Why do we watch all the hurt
and do nothing?

Those who do something
To ease the pain

Can get punished

Those who do something
To ease the pain
Can get praised

It's a random gamble
Because we can only control
Our own actions

Pain can be used as a lesson
Pain can be used as a weapon
We get to choose sides

Smear

Thank you for smearing my name
Letting all know how you play the game
Your heart's untrue
You're no pal
You're no confidante

And if I dare unmask you
Just imagine what you'll put me through
I'll see you and then your flying monkeys too
Working hard to attack me
Thank you for smearing my name

Nothing

What comes to mind
When one has nothing to say?
Will it be something kind
Or will silence rule the day?

Mindfulness speaks
When we breathe in and out
Truthfulness wreaks
When we let our actions shout

Someone hurt me
I was advised to do nothing
Do nothing; let it be
Whatever the emotions bring

Emotions are bringing words
Turned into poetry
Instead of slinging swords
Slinging creativity

Blind Loyalty

There's a lot to be said
About blind loyalty
It's a noble, desirable,
Achievable quality

Are you willing to
Corrupt yourself for it?
Are you willing to
Change who you are?

To whom are you blindly loyal?
To yourself?
To a person?
To a cause?
To ascension?

You won't find your answer
In this poem
The answer to those questions
Lie within you

To whom are you blindly loyal?

Finding Self

When finding yourself
Where do you look?
If you suddenly realize
That you've been mistook

That someone has projected
Themselves onto you
Then tried to manipulate
The false to be true

Just give yourself time
Be gentle and kind
Your core doesn't change
You'll find it engage

When you love yourself
And love yourself first
Accept the best parts of you
Accept all the worst

Learn to do better
Day after day
And to finding yourself
You will learn the way

Once a Day

Challenge yourself
Once a day
Seek adventure
Come what may

Write a poem
If you dare
Or something else
To show you care

Find some growth
But be aware
That sometimes growth
Can give a scare

See it through
And do your best
Then you can earn
Some deserved rest

Gaps

The pressure to write
Doesn't seem to help
The process

It's the irony
Of the Universe

Thinking that poetry
Has rules when
Creation is generally found
In the gaps

Find the gaps
And fill them
Or they will be filled for you

There are words that don't fully describe
What one means to say
Because there is always a gap in understanding

As much as I can convey with words
Actions and expressions
A gap remains between us

Find the gaps

And fill them
Hopefully with good things

Eleven

This is the eleventh poem in this book
There are eleven syllables in this line
This poem will have eleven lines to it
Each line uses the word eleven some way
Is eleven an odd number used often?
Meta analyzing about eleven…
Two number ones combined make up eleven
How many more "Eleven" lines are left, now?
Three more lines until eleven lines are reached
Meta analyzing this "Eleven" poem
And the last line has to end with "eleven".

Falling Behind

Falling behind is ok
As long as you don't give up
On commitments made
Especially to yourself

The process is often more challenging
Than previously expected
Probabilities favor consistency over luck
Work on consistency and hope for luck

Don't give up. Look up.
See if falling behind is what was meant to be
Maybe another path is meant to be
And falling behind was a sign towards
something else

Commitment

What does commitment look like?
What does it feel like?
A burning in the chest?
A focus in the eyes?

How long does commitment last?
It lasts as long as you have
The desire to achieve your goals.

What are your goals?
What are you committed to doing?

Balance

Balance can be hard and easy
When learning it can be tough
When experienced, can be fun
Achieving balance is a worthy challenge
Of yourself.
Find balance within yourself.
You control it.

Untitled

Flowers and plants breathe.
Do they know that we
Are aware of them?
What would they do
If they knew about us?

Animals breathe, too.
We are animals.
Evolved and still not.
Why do we still hate?
What can't we accept?

Diversity is.
Equity is, too.
Inclusion, one more.
The ending of hate;
Acceptance begins.

Seek Struggle

Struggle is often seen and cast
In a sad and negative light
When spoken of in such down ways
It can produce a fright

Struggle is a path to growth
To those who understand
Important growth can only win
When seeking to understand

Comfort is ok too sometimes and
Well deserved with rest
It will not bring you what you want
For struggles win the test

Seventeen

I was seventeen
Exactly 30 years ago.
So much has passed,
So much to know,
Yet so much more
To go.

At seventeen,
I felt so old and
Ready for the world
The future lay
Ahead of me
So much to be unfurled.

A performer I became.
Creating stage works, too.
Someone answering a phone
You may have called into.

A lawyer in the courts
Is what I came to be
Until the time I realized
There's so much more to see

Thirty more years to

Seventy-seven.
If I don't make it there,
I hope I make it to heaven

Rule

Why respect the rule of law
When the ones on power don't?
Why continue following
When opportunists won't?

It seems we need to be like them
In order to succeed
But all the while we know that there's
A better way to lead

Why wait for revolution
Before engaging change?
It's 'cuz the ones in power
Don't need to rearrange

Can we correct ourselves
Before this gets to worst?
It all depends on whether we
see rules or fight for first.

Unbounded

I once believed
I was good at seeing
All sides of a bounded circumstance
Of which I was not involved

By contrast I was bad
At seeing clearly all sides
Of circumstances involving me

I believe this is because
I am unbounded and
Therefore can
Achieve and sustain anything

Circumstances that involve me
Also involve an element of my control
Which I mold to fit the circumstance
And towards the best outcome for all

This causes me to mold myself
To conform to the circumstance that
Helps everyone else and serves me last
Which I'm learning needs to change

For I am bounded too

I am bounded by my own physical limitations
My own emotional and mental needs
My boundaries exists whether I acknowledge
them or not

Untitled

What happens when one
Cannot tell
The victim from
The abuser?

Trust your gut
Listen and look
The truth doesn't ask you
To believe it

Some abusers have
Learned very well
How to play
The victim

We all learn from abusers
May we all not have to
Suffer from them
Or become them out of necessity

Yourself

Find yourself
In the air
In between
In your breath

Move yourself
Through the air
Through space and time
Through moments passed

Be yourself
Take up air
Take up space
Take up life

www.ingramcontent.com/pod-product-compliance
Lightning Source LLC
LaVergne TN
LVHW010952200726
843509LV00013B/2378